Kaitlyn Jane Mauro

"We do not see the world as it is,
we see it as we are."
- *Unknown*

Kaitlyn Jane Mauro

Inhale, exhale.

From my old diaries and the cracks in the walls.
It only took me eighteen years.

ISBN-10: 1450551696
EAN-13: 9781450551694

Cover photography by Brittney Lewis.
Cover design by the author.

Kaitlyn Jane Mauro

One Six Billionth

By Kaitlyn Jane Mauro

Kaitlyn Jane Mauro

My first book is dedicated to all
the people I've met along the way.

-

'Nothing of me is original,
I am the combined effort of
everyone I have ever known.'
- Chuck Palahniuk

Kaitlyn Jane Mauro

Introduction-
Ready, set, go.

    I took an introduction to college writing class not long ago. One afternoon, while the class was having a difficult time coming up with topics for our definition papers, the professor gave us some advice that has really stuck with me. 'Some people believe to write about something you must already know exactly how you feel about it. I think we don't really know how we feel about something *until* we try to write about it.' Write what you know, they tell us. She also advised us not to write about love or music because you can't do either without sounding like a fruitcake. I have written about both in these pages, hopefully she'll forgive me.

    Books have always been my escape, writing my release - my way of breaking down and understanding things. Let's analyze the handwriting, let's look for the patterns. I'm in love with a Maya Angelou quote that reads something like, 'When people tell you who they are, believe them the first time.' Read between my lines. Reading back through all the notebooks I've kept over the years has been a strange journey. They say if you want to see someone's future, look to their past. Like most things in life, this contains a dose of truth but not the complete picture. I have to believe we have the option to change who we are and where we are going, anytime. This is what gives us room to hope. Every breath has the potential to begin a new era.

Boom da da da da da boom dat dat da da.

My life feels like endless fresh starts without any real conclusions. There are so many childish vows I make with myself. I'm forever planning to change my habits; to break the bad ones and adopt fresh, new rhythms to live by. Let's read the news every morning so we'll feel connected to the world and always have something relevant to say. Let's live off fresh fruit and mugs of coffee, warming us from our cores and giving us the energy to do. Accomplish accomplish accomplish. That seems to be everyone's mantra this year - but in eighty years we'll all be planted in the ground like the flowers and what will become of all our important accomplishments then? Our lives are specks of dust wasted in worry. Only one six billionth of it is about you. Does that make you feel free? Thinking like this makes me feel reckless, light-hearted, and young. Like wearing piles of opulent jewelry without a special occasion or spontaneously kissing someone in the middle of a sentence, any ordinary sentence. 'How do you take your coffee?'

Emerson said, 'Do not be timid about your actions. All life is an experiment.' I want to adopt the habit of always following through, always doing what I say I will - even the random, trivial little promises I make constantly without a thought. Tie up all the loose ends of life, but what would be the point of that? Life is supposed to be messy. Being human means you will get your heart broken and your fingernails dirty.

'Clutter and mess show that life is being lived. Clutter is wonderfully fertile ground – you can still discover new things under all those piles, clean things up, edit things out, fix things, get a grip. Tidiness suggests that something is as good as it is going to get. Tidiness makes me think of held breath, of suspended animation.'
(Anne Lamott)

A quote from my all time favorite book, *Bird By Bird*. I've loved it since I was thirteen. An interim pastor at the church where I grew up recommended it to me. My copy has been read and carried around in my purse so many times the front cover has literally been worn off. I've made notes and doodled in most of the corners and margins. Various sentences and even whole paragraphs are underlined and bracketed with the ink of a hundred borrowed pens. Lines I want to remember, lines that feel especially authentic or poignant. Absolute creative disarray. C'est la vie, right?

> 'Perfection is shallow, unreal,
> and fatally uninteresting.'
> (Anne Lamott)

Another of my favorite *Bird By Bird* lines. Editing is my favorite part of the process - polishing, shading, and fine-tuning. I've always had a thing for words, savoring my attempts to create something artistic. Language is so generally unappreciated; permeating every aspect of our lives but rarely given a moment's thought. We take our words for granted - throwing them around as though they are weightless and worthless. We don't put in the effort to speak beautifully - anything close to the point will do. Talk is cheap. I'm guilty of this crime too. I say things just to hear myself speak. I say ugly things I don't mean. Sometimes I regret my words but most of the time I barely remember what I've said and they go the way of everything else, lost to history. Everything belongs to the earth, to the dirt and the dust. Everything we have, from our breath down to our bones, is only borrowed. When I'm weaving lines together on the page things are different. These consonants and vowels are my inks and my palette. I trade them in and out of a sentence until I find the right rhythm, capture the exact feeling I want to convey. Most of the time I start writing without so much to say and I end up surprised by the words that show up at my fingertips, strung together like glass beads, aching to escape to the page where they can breath.

Writing is both very natural and very difficult. I can't think of a clever analogy for it. Ideas, lines, and stories loop inside my mind like a cassette tape all day but when I sit down to capture them, to tame and arrange them into some semblance of sensible order my thoughts become gauzy and muted. I see the vaguest shapes of things but nothing sharp or discernable. The jungle drums start to beat. The words are elusive – like someone's name on the tip of your tongue. If only I had learned to achieve this sort of mental nothingness several years ago when I was trying to take up mediation.

I hear similar sentiments from other writers, even quite successful writers whose work you've probably seen on the shelves of bookstores and libraries or maybe even read. It's a panic stricken feeling of having lost your touch, of being a has-been before you've even begun. People are going to realize you are boring, that you have no original thoughts. Everything you ever penned that was mildly interesting was a stroke of beginner's luck. Your mother is the only one who will bother to read your book. You consider pouring your mug of coffee (or possibly herbal tea if you are trying to lower your caffeine intake, as per your therapists suggestions) over everything you have just created – just to be entirely sure nobody will ever be subjected to reading your horrible first drafts ever again. God forbid you are killed in an accident and someone reads your files and realizes you really are, in fact, an untalented, cliché, carbon copy person. The worst kind of fake. They'd tell everyone! I think most writers secretly feel like frauds, even when they see their names in print.

Writing for publication is ironic - writers are isolated, in solitary confinement with their thoughts but at the same time writing is all about reaching people. Writing gives you a reason to look more closely at life, to let yourself really feel and pay attention. Writing is taking notes, making it all more significant. It's choosing, through the act of isolation, to be public. It's putting yourself out there, exposed in the world where anyone can see and snap pictures. It's letting yourself be a little vulnerable in exchange for a voice and the chance to be heard.

'Speak the truth, even if your voice shakes'
(Maggie Kuhn)

The wonderful part is you can be heard without ever actually having to stand in front of the crowds and speak. You can go back and edit everything again and again before anyone sees it, taking out the um's and the awkward pauses to make it all sound more intelligent. I hate only having one shot to get something right, I'm a big fan of adjusting things.

I've written online under a nom de plume for years but that's a very different game. I can say whatever I want and it doesn't matter who reads it or how much they disagree with everything I stand for because, for all intents and purposes, it's not connected to me. It's like the Post Secret project – there is a comfortable sense of liberation in confessing your secrets and shames to strangers. There's validation to be found in learning other people's counterfeits and realizing everyone really is just as confused and dysfunctional as you. If you still think they are likeable even with their flaws and emotional baggage then maybe you aren't so unlovable either, after all. It's one lovely revelation. We're all just human, made of the same bones and heartbeats. We're all flaws stitched together with mostly good intentions. I wonder what would happen if everyone just said whatever it is they are trying so hard not to say. Mass chaos most likely, do you disagree? I'd tell you that I love you. It's different when your name is printed along the spine.

Kaitlyn Jane Mauro

Escapism.

"Man is least himself when he talks in his own person. Give him a mask, and he will tell you the truth."
- Oscar Wilde

There is a word from my psychology class: schema, which means the conceptual models we create in our minds to understand the world. We try to comprehend each new experience by what we already know, fitting it in with what we've already experienced. This process is called assimilation. But if we can't make it fit into what we believe then it changes us and forces us to adapt our beliefs, to adjust our perspectives to hold the new information.

We spend our entire lives learning and relearning what is true of the world.

After eighteen years I'm done searching for myself. We paint our identities with the choices we make and the way we see the world. Our perspectives are what define us. I would say we also paint our own destinies but having a mother who was diagnosed with cancer makes you rethink things like this. You cannot find some higher meaning or purpose in everything, sometimes shit just happens.

We don't find ourselves in some ultimate 'ah-hah' moment. Life is full of little epiphanies and fragments of inspiration. Everyone has their own set of truths. We use them like moral GPS systems, trying to make sense of human behavior and the things that happen to us.

I don't understand people who believe so stubbornly that their way of doing things is the only right way, their beliefs the only truths. Closed mindedness is the swiftest way to make me dislike you. I try not to judge people's choices, pretty much following the rule of 'as long as you aren't hurting anyone do whatever makes you happy'. If you want to pray to Allah or Buddha or Mother Nature or Edward Cullen, go right ahead. If you want to sleep with other men or kiss other women, that's entirely your choice. If you choose to stay single all of your life or fall in love twice each time you go to the grocery store, by all means - knock yourself out. Whether you believe the world was a big accident or that it's God's masterpiece, you have the right to your own opinions. If you choose to chase fame, money, or enlightenment; to live in Beverly Hills, or a cave, or a hippie commune – to each his own. Who is anyone else to tell you how to live your life?

I am in love with sunrises and the stars. I call them my constants. Sometimes I get restless because I really need to see the stars and it's cloudy for days. When I see the sun rising or the dark sky filled with constellations it feels like someone has kept a promise to me. These are guaranteed events, something that can be counted on to happen no matter where I am or how fucked up my life feels at the moment. 'Death and taxes' they say, but I like this better.

Kaitlyn Jane Mauro

Ne Me Quitte Pas Mon Cher,

I'm sitting in one of my favorite places right now: the big beautiful Carnegie Library in the city. It has both a calming and energizing effect on me. I leave with books stacked in my arms nearly up to my chin, feeling giddy and inspired (if slightly overwhelmed). There is so much knowledge within these walls. So many stories, perspectives, angles, and lives - you could spend your entire lifetime here and never run out of new concepts. I absolutely adore this place, where people whisper their conversations and the walls of shelves stretch above and beneath you for stories and stories. The floors are made of glass tiles and you can see the shadows of people walking in the aisles above you. The whole place feels almost sacred to me.

This is where I belong, I just know it. Somewhere among these pages - my work and life and heart on a shelf, with a tidy little cover and page numbers to make it official, tangible. I become restless if I go too long without new books to make me grow. I will write only for art. I want to be so eccentric and genuine. Yet this waste of a school year looms and the cookie cutter college experience waits at the end of it. Everything on the horizon looks so conventional and planned. I want to do something a little crazy, something radical and spontaneous. I want to run away to Ireland or Paris. It all used to excite me, now I just dread it. I need to get so much work done and I need to start so many applications.

Tick tock tick tock, constantly reminded of what is at stake, of the fact that time is loosening and running out like sand through my parted fingers. I am young I am young I am young. I carry a piece of petrified wood from the Painted Dessert of New Mexico in my wallet. It is millions of years old, reminding of how young we all are. In the big picture, human beings never really become old. Our lives are so short when you really think about it. They are flashes of lightening - here and then gone, barely there and not remembered for long. The most we can hope for is that some small piece of our work might remain and be passed down through the generations.

I am constant. I am breathing. I really need to center myself, maybe I should start doing yoga or something. I can't stand being in my own head lately, trapped in with my thoughts like a relentless stereo, too loud. It hurts my eardrums. I need constant change, constant movement, new ideas and inspiration. 'Love is the answer to a question that I have forgotten'. Oh Regina Spektor, sing me some cinnamon and old time jazz.

I, I, I, I, I - what an exhausting little letter.

'A love affair with this world', they said it in church like it was such a terrible thing. I think it's poetic and beautiful, if a little broken. I want to have a love affair with this world. I can picture my life 10 years from now. I'm probably still a lot like I am now - just older, worldlier. Hopefully I've seen more of the world. Maybe I have a love or maybe I've lost him, letting him slip through my fingers. Maybe I still haven't found him. Maybe I've fallen a hundred times. It never gets old.

Bruised or broken, at first it's so hard to tell. All pain feels the same, numbing. There is no way to know until you put some time and space into the mix. Let it all thin itself out. I am such a love junkie. I can picture you though. The way it will feel when our eyes meet. Private smiles, our own little jokes. You'll keep me from swinging too far, we'll waste a lot of time thinking up questions and making plans. You'll tell me to just shut up and breath when I start picturing my car tangled up in the trees. You'll be a traveler too and we'll sip coffee and debate everything. Two seekers like us could have one hell of a love affair. Maybe it will last forever and maybe it won't but my god, somewhere in the middle there we will have really tried.

Maybe I'll work in nonexistence, in stories and characters and words nobody else can hear or see. I'll give them form and texture. Shades and hues and grain - it's all an illusion, that's what makes it art. I'll spend my days moving behind the stacks of books and pages, living in constant inspiration, seeking out things that starve me and make me feel alive. My heart was broken this past weekend, did you know that? For the first time, but probably not the last. I digress. I will still drink too much coffee and probably have cupboards full of teacups and no grapefruit spoons. I'll probably still be a pretty big mess but I will smile and I'll still stop my car on the side of the road and fall in love with the autumn colors. I will still close my eyes and imagine the applause is for me when I walk up the aisle, leaving the theater early to go find my car and beat the traffic. I'll still wish I had picked up ballet or languages sooner, I might have become good at something, found my niche. Maybe I'll be religious, maybe I will give it up. I'll always whisper prayers in my desperate moments, even if I don't exactly know who I am talking to. I'll have African violets and mismatched fabrics.

I am a Jackson Pollock kind of girl. His paintings are always my favorite. My uncle pointed this out to me at his arts school in St Louis this past weekend. 'You take your coffee black, that's my kind of girl,' the sweetest old man said this to me while I was working in the café last weekend, a complete stranger. I love sweet old men, they can be so charming. The smallest things can make my day. Sometimes walking in crowds makes me feel lonely, other times it is just what I need: companionship, even if it's completely impersonal.

I heard that to speak a second language is to have a second soul.

Open your eyes, art is everywhere.

'Nothing is original. Steal from anywhere that resonates with inspiration or fuels your imagination. Devour old films, new films, music, books, paintings, photographs, poems, dreams, random conversations, architecture, bridges, street signs, trees, clouds, bodies of water, light and shadows. Select only things to steal from that speak directly to your soul. If you do this, your work (and theft) will be authentic. Authenticity is invaluable; originality is non-existent. And don't bother concealing your thievery - celebrate it if you feel like it.' *-Jim Jarmusch*

I absolutely love that quote. Inspiration should be absorbed, borrowed, and breathed wherever it's found. The things that inspire you will shape you and your art. 'Authenticity is invaluable; originality is non-existent' - my favorite line. It's incredibly humbling to realize none of our thoughts or feelings are really all that original after all. It's all been felt before. Perspective, by definition, means the things nearest to you look bigger than they are - distorted, disproportionate. It happens in photography and in love. People have been fighting these same battles and wrestling with these same questions since the very beginning.

I love random questions and facts about people. Here's one for you now. I'm a halfway decent liar. I do it sometimes for amusement, making up characters to be for strangers. I like pretending to be someone completely made up when I sit next to strangers on planes. It's really all just a game.

Each generation thinks they are so revolutionary - they are going to do everything so differently, change the world entirely. Yet sometimes the sheer apathy of people makes me sick for the world. I contradict myself. Sometimes I can't bring myself to read the news because it feels like the sky is falling and how can I possibly function when that is going on? Sometimes it's necessary to stick your head in the sand, this is what selective memory is for. I hate how some people are so willing to settle, to exist rather than live, to let life become a chore and to let themselves be ordinary. To do something requires risking the illusions we have grown so comfortable with, it involves sticking your neck out a little sometimes. It's a lot like falling in love. Everything always comes back to love, doesn't it? I am a hopeless romantic with a cynical sense of humor. I've been told I am too jaded for my eighteen years.

'Life has been your art.
You have set yourself to music.
Your days are your sonnets.'
(Oscar Wilde)

What a concept, no? One of the most inspiring people I know is a friend I've had for several years. We happened by chance and looking back it's so unlikely that we met at all. She lives on the west coast, right up against the Pacific Ocean. I'm infinitely jealous of this. I'll live near the sea someday. People seem so much more creative there, like the untamed vastness of the tides and currents keeps them hungry for life.

Apparently there are more independently published authors in California than any other state.

She is one of the most alive, interesting, lovely people I know. When we met it was like I'd found someone running on the same wavelength or living in the same language I was. She encourages me to seek out the spice in life, to look for the beauty and have the courage to risk making a mess of things. She reminds me that being a little broken and incredibly human can still be a beautiful thing. She is the most romantic and creative of my friends.

We write letters, it's our main form of communication. It feels almost timeless to me. There really isn't anything so rare about sending letters but hardly anyone does it anymore. I don't like how efficient and cold email and text messaging is. No finger prints. It lacks warmth and commitment - letters say 'I took the time to write all this out and put a stamp on it just for you'. Love letters are such a dying art.

The way we write letters might be a little on the eccentric side. We decorate the envelopes with iridescent nail polish and cut out magazine words. We send little things along, tucked in with our stationary: polaroid pictures, teas, origami cranes, rings, candy, beads, charms, seashells, mix cds, drawings. Anything to keep it interesting.

I don't buy packs of stamps because I secretly love making trips to the post office to send things. Most people think of it as an errand but it feels decadent to me somehow. I like chatting with the charming old men while I stand in line. I wish I could travel as easily as my words do.

Kaitlyn Jane Mauro

My thoughts and these pages are all out of order.
No comment.

Kaitlyn Jane Mauro

The only religion I still believe in is love.

If you get down to the heart of it nobody really knows what comes next. Death is supposed to be the final, grand closing of the stage curtains but there are hundreds of theories about what happens after. Truths are handed out like calling cards in Vegas, where the streets are literally lined with porn. It's marvelously trashy. This reminds me of a man my sister and I met at the Grand Canyon. Seven thousand feet above the earth, we're on top of the world and he's handing out little purple leaflets: *'Repent or burn eternally in hell!'*. We are standing on top of the

Grand Canyon (the *Grand Canyon*) while the sun is setting - the sky looks like it's on fire and somehow this man thinks if we don't see God in this overwhelmingly beautiful place his cartoon will open our eyes. Open our eyes and save our souls. People were avoiding him, averting their gazes. He made everyone uncomfortable, even the Christians. It's laughable that anyone thinks this is effective. Everyone thinks everyone else is living life with blinkers on. So it goes.

We believe what makes us comfortable. I used to spend a lot of time debating questions that have no answers. Wondering where we were before our heartbeats started, why we are here, where we go when we die. Sometimes I feel like the questions are more important than the answers anyway.

'You don't have a soul,
you are a soul.
You have a body.'
(C.S. Lewis)

I've gone to church since I was born but after eighteen winters, springs, autumns, and summers I think I am done. It's not that I don't believe in God anymore - more that my definition of God has expanded and the traditions and rules of church feel suffocating. They don't make sense to me anymore. I certainly still believe there is some kind of God who created the world and hears people when they pray. I look around me and everything seems like a miracle, there is no way all of this happened by accident. Chemicals don't spontaneously explode and create something this intricate and perfectly balanced. Study the human body, every inch functions in more sophisticated ways than we can begin to comprehend. Science is ever proving us children.

'We are not humans having spiritual experiences, we are spiritual beings having human experiences.'
(Teilhard de Chardin)

I see God in nature, in the fact that every time I look up at the sky it's different. I see God in the fact that we're here at all and in the way the flowers somehow know when to come up in the spring. I see God in the fact that we don't know where the universe ends and we can't even begin to count the stars. I sometimes see God in the people I know. Call God a her or call God a him, it really couldn't matter less.

I recognize God in many different religions, like a common thread woven and painted by different cultures until the familiar is nearly unrecognizable - but it's there, the same quintessence in every corner of the world. I can worship just as well in a synagogue or a Hindu temple as in a protestant church. It's not God that is different - it's the packaging. It's the people and the culture. This is what I have come to believe. Learn as much as you can, keep an open mind, then form your own opinions. That's the only way to do things. I am not deluded enough to think I have the answers.

To be fair, I have met some lovely, genuine people in church. People who really try to live what they preach and do right in their lives. I've also met a lot of hypocrites. *A lot* of hypocrites. I don't pretend to be above them; I've been among the stone throwers more often than I've been the accused. I've heard people gossiping with harsh words and the coldest of hearts. I've seen power struggles and popularity games similar to those perpetrated by junior high school girls. Judgment, intolerance, power trips, self-righteousness, cliques, greed, social climbing, dishonesty, favoritism, and exclusion - all in churches. There are miserable people who go to church and miserable people who don't, good people who are religious and good people who aren't. It all comes back to the bottom line: there isn't a person here who isn't human. Still, I feel like church isn't what it was designed to be. They tell me the world is fallen and I suppose it's true. People are just people where ever you go.

Whichever theory about God turns out to be true is fine with me. That being said, one thing is for sure - if there is some ultimate after party when we die, Christopher McCandless is the first person I want to meet.

-

I have been astonished that men could die martyrs for religion - I have shuddered at it. I shudder no more - I could be martyred for my religion - Love is my religion - I could die for that.
(John Keats)

'As you go.'

our lips touch dainty teacups
as fragile and breakable as
the air around us
as our conversation
sipping sweet, wild orange tea
my favorite:
you always were and still are.
my piano melodies
let's hum gently along
background music for my mind
another constant
like my pulse and the stars
filling the empty spaces
leaving no room to need you
try to pacify the emptiness.
but he's the ghost of a heartbeat
caged; too strong in my chest
reminding me where I am,
of risky behavior and
laughing until everything fades.
he's my one million clichés
but I never learned the art of a light switch heart.
inhale, exhale, speak.
our eyes meet, breathe
he glances away, breaks the contact
always hungry
always starving
those are the rules of our game

say something, anything
thoughtless, sporadic
he abuses each word
taking advantage of each sound
time slips through my fingertips
so fast the heart aches
it feels like homesickness
then he is gone
and it feels so familiar
every time
feral, urgent
numbness seeps deeper within
with each stroke becoming
as ingrained as the words on my wrist.
don't hold on, don't need
don't want, don't speak
'don't be weak'
he tells me
strong hands on my shoulders
the truth will not set you free,
the truth will not set you free.
and I find myself alone
with only the entire world
a forgotten trinket you left behind
and a slightly less innocent heart
for company,
as you go.

Kaitlyn Jane Mauro

Life A La Mode.

I read somewhere that you should try to do one thing each day that scares you – some days I remember to do this. Occasionally I feel like getting out of bed at all should count. I remember how miraculous it is that I'm here at all and I take solace in the fact that so far I have survived everything.

Last weekend I sang a little solo in church. I was pretty nervous beforehand. Lately I tend to speak in whispers. A friend pointed out to me that I've been trailing off at the end of my sentences and mumbling the last few words. I hadn't noticed. What a strange habit to pick up. 'Sing a solo' was on the life list I started years ago. There are so many things I want to experience. I think about my future a lot, about where I will live and how I will spend my time, about all the places I want to see and what a wild, eccentric old lady I will be someday. I'll listen to loud music and flirt with the grocery store clerks. I'll call everyone 'darling' or 'honey' or 'sugar. I'll have books stacked on every surface, slip easily between languages, and always be learning about something new. I'll know all the waitresses by name and bake banana bread for my mailman at Christmas. Maybe I'll move someplace new every few months, never get settled enough to become too bored or lonely. Thinking about the future helps me feel less overwhelmed by the present.

A boy I used to work with messaged me last night completely out of the blue. I've always thought he was rather good looking but aside from small talk while we did our jobs we've never had much conversation. 'I want to travel' he says. Wanderlust, it's one of my favorite words. Ambivalence, iridescent, airy, darling, ethereal, library. 'Okay, let's go backpack through Europe and jump trains' I tell him, wondering if maybe he's been drinking or something. It just seemed so random. He hadn't been – I guess he just remembered me talking about traveling a lot at work or something. We ended up talking for two hours, planning this theoretical backpacking trip. We'll go to Ireland and Spain and Germany and stay in hostels and the ice hotel. We joked about the topless beaches in Brazil. He read the 'life list' and two poems I'd posted in the notes section of my facebook profile. He asked me if I knew I was very interesting, which made me smile for about half an hour. We talked about religion and Into The Wild, which is pretty much my favorite movie of all time. It's such a shame he's a republican who hates coffee... but maybe these things really don't matter that much. It's funny how people you think you know can completely surprise you.

Some things from my 'life list'...

~~Take a cross-country road trip~~. Become an expert at something. Go dog sledding. Go skinny-dipping. ~~Watch the sunset at the Grand Canyon~~. ~~See the castles along the Rhine River~~. Drink wine in France. See wild elephants. Float in the Dead Sea. See the huge Koi fish in Japan. Visit the cities where Jesus walked. See the Taj Mahal. Pick fruit and bake a pie. See the Eiffel Tower.

Ride an elephant in India. Visit a psychic. Become fluent in Spanish. Learn French. Swim with dolphins. Give away everything I own. Take a train ride through England. Learn Italian. See a wild Orca. Ireland. ~~Paint a mural~~. Eat gelato in Rome. Kiss a stranger. Visit a natural hot spring. Explore a volcano. Get incredibly hung over. Go cliff diving. Learn to play an instrument. See Victoria Falls. See the Great Pyramids. Donate blood. Stay someplace haunted. Go skydiving. ~~Sing a solo~~. ~~Become an author~~. ~~Get a tattoo~~. Adopt a child. Go white water rafting. Fall in love. Elope. Ride in a hot air balloon. ~~New York City~~. Graduate from college. ~~Visit the White House~~. Go backpacking. Be an extra in a movie. Go to all 50 states. Walk along the Great Wall of China. Spend a year helping people. See the northern lights. Learn to dance. Study photography. Grow a flower garden. Greece.

Wow. I'd better get busy.

I think I have been to twenty two of the fifty states so far, I just tried to count them off on my fingers. So much traveling left to do, even within the borders of my own country. If I had a car I would just wake up one morning and decide to take a spontaneous trip to New York

City or Boston or the ocean. Someday I will do these things.

Kaitlyn Jane Mauro

Oh wow, lovely.

Brittany Murphy died today. It was cardiac arrest and a lot of people are making speculations, saying it was probably drugs that killed her. It's all just gossip and will remain a mystery for a while. Apparently these toxicology reports can take months, CSI makes it look so efficient - instant gratification crime solving. I would never want a job that reminded me of my own mortality everyday. Nobody close to me has ever died young or died tragically (knock on wood). I've been to the funerals of my great grandmothers but it's a mixed sense of sadness, loss, and some kind of joy in the mourning there.

Almost like a sense of completion. They both lived long, interesting lives - well into their nineties and both very sick at the end. They had become empty shells of who they once were. Back around the full circle of life to the indignity and helplessness where we began - comme des enfants, like children. Nobody liked seeing them like that. It's different when the person is young and there is so much lost opportunity and potential. It feels like something was stolen from them and from everyone left behind.

Brittany was so beautiful; I've always liked her movies and the happy go lucky characters she played. I remember when I first saw Little Black Book and it made me fall in love with Carly Simon's music. Her character was laying on the bathroom floor singing, an absolute mess of a person. The character's flaws made her incredibly likeable. It feels like unglamorous things like death shouldn't happen to people as beautiful as Brittany. Death in movies is graceful, heroic. This all sounds dumb, even to me. She was always so alive and energetic on screen. I admired her big eyes and the awkward charm of her characters. I wonder if her movies will become a fresh trend now that she is gone. Everyone thought Michael Jackson was a creep until he died, though very few will admit it now.

People are so indignant. Instead they print tee shirts and tote bags with his face on them and say he changed the world. So it goes.

A football player from one of the local high schools died last year. Apparently he just collapsed during football practice one day, nobody knew there as anything wrong with him. Then he's gone. It was his heart, if I remember correctly. I used to spend so much time in that area when it was all still only a 67F bus ride away. I really enjoyed the hours of independence and the easy, undemanding company of the other strangers in the library or the cafes - reading and sipping our coffee drinks. I was surprised by how much his death bothered me since I hadn't even known him. For weeks after I heard the news I had dreams about this boy I'd never met. I read all the articles about him they published in the local papers, I don't know why I was so intrigued.

I used to see lots of kids from his school waiting at the bus stops along Main Street in the afternoons when I would be waiting for the 67F. We'd stand at the stops together in silence, together yet apart. Sometimes I'd make small talk with one of them - the boys in their ties and khaki pants, the girls in their navy sweaters and plaid skirts. I have this thing about talking to strangers, I love to be reminded of how many people there are in the world. It makes my problems seem less important, it makes ending up lonely seem far less likely. I saw a picture of him and weeded through my memory, trying to remember if I had ever seen him there. Maybe we had exchanged smiles or glances.

They say death makes life important. I suppose that is probably true. If there's nothing at stake then what is the point? We need to feel like somebody is watching what we do for it to have meaning. I think we all secretly feel like the exception, the one that's going to get out alive. But the truth is nobody is going to get out alive. We need to live our lives unafraid and hungry, we need to stop being afraid of not being enough or not making the right impressions. Be afraid of wasted time and of missing things. Be afraid of turning life into a to do list and missing all the scenery outside the train window. The beautiful thing is that most wrong choices can be corrected by simply making another decision. This is definitely not true for certain things but for some situations it is a comforting thing to remember.

I had a boyfriend who used to laugh at me because when I would get really stressed I would start to say 'eighty years - we'll all be dead' to myself. He thought this was terribly morbid and depressing but I think it might be one of the most inspiring thing I've ever heard. Be terribly human and terribly alive. Make a fool of yourself. Find something that lights you on fire.

-

'Don't ask what the world needs. Ask what makes you come alive, and go do it. Because what the world needs is people who have come alive.'
(Howard Thurman)

Kaitlyn Jane Mauro

Bad love poems are everywhere.

I heard the opposite of love isn't hate it's indifference. If there is still anger or hurt someone holds the power. Once you stop caring the game is over. It's nearly four a.m. and I still haven't gone to sleep. Tomorrow starts a new era but tonight I'm haunted by my memories. Waves of loss sneak up on me and drag me down under. Breathing becomes something I have to remember to do, like a skill I haven't mastered. Little clips of our love play in my mind like old home videos, emotions magnified. Things weren't supposed to end this way, I wanted you to be my exception. Friends and lovers leave but life stops for no one. We linger on.

Up all night got demons to fight - I want to rid you from my bones. After two years we've come to this last stage. We've been talked out of our feelings and things have been different for too long, there is nothing to come back to. At last, there is nothing left to say. Confabulation runs deep in our veins, we rewrite our histories and color our memories. Change is the only thing we are promised.

We aren't guaranteed a proper ending or even the chance to say goodbye. All we have is right now.

When you fall in love you get used to seeing a special recognition in the person's eyes and even when you're fighting it's still there. When it's all over and you look and don't find that familiar something anymore you discover it's a stranger looking back at you. I've always thought this is the most painful part. It will shake you to the core if you let it. Inhale, exhale. Distraction is beautiful. Burning his things might also help.

I wish there were more words for love in our language. I hate that the meaning becomes so casual and worn out. Some words should remain sacred, for the most special of moments. Read between my lines. As it turns out, there isn't a soul in this world you can't live without. Love is a drug, running through our body and leaving us dependant. The withdrawal is a bitch but I'm finally sober of my past. Rose colored goggles off - but sometimes it's not so terrible to see things as more significant than they are.

I like to think of myself as constantly evolving, constantly seeking. Reading through my old diaries is strange. I feel like I'm intruding - reading the thoughts and secrets of someone I no longer recognize. I wonder if someday reading these pages will give me that feeling. It's crazy to think that the new year is here - this year that will hold so many transitions for my friends and I. Sometimes I still feel very much like a child.

I like to wonder about all the people that came before me, I wonder what we had in common. It's amazing to think about how each one had to fall in love with a specific person at a specific time, all the stars that had to align so we could be here. Things could have turned out so differently, we've already beat the odds just by being here.

Impact.

I had my first car accident today. It was over so fast. I barely remember what happened but I remember the feeling of the car spinning out of control on the black ice. My stomach disappeared into thin air as I realized I had no control over anything. The impact as my side of the car plowed into the wooden rails was incredible and quite scary. I felt jumpy and distracted for the rest of the day. Of course I was freaking out so after I called my Dad to come help me get the car out the first thing I did was text Cory. He's so steady most of the time, I love it. Sometimes I'm so wildly inconsistent. Even my handwriting is indecisive, completely different from one line to the next. I think we balance each other out.

Ever since the days of Adam we have been hiding from God then saying 'God is hard to find'.

A quote by Fulton J Sheen. I have been reading about other religions lately. I love how Buddhism has such a philosophical angle to it. I really respect religions that practice tolerance and open mindedness. Wars should never be fought over spiritual things, it's so hypocritical. I read about a concept in Jainism last night called Kshamavani Parva. I have no idea how to pronounce this but it looks beautiful typed out on the page. Apparently it's a day when everyone goes around and asking forgiveness for all of the wrongs they have committed - intentionally or otherwise. I wish I could do this in my own life, it seems like a wonderful way to clear your conscience and become more humble.

It's funny how so often we walk around like we are apologizing for our very existence, mumbling 'sorry' when we walk in front of anyone or breath. We say it so much it loses its meaning, becoming only sounds strung together in a breath, but when we really owe someone an apology we can barely bring ourselves to mutter the words. Everybody craves a second chance and a fresh start.

Of course, the flipside of wanting a clean slate is that you have to forgive all the horrible, tiny people who have wronged you too. This is the fly in the ointment. Grudges will weigh you down, sucking away at your energy and your happiness. Again I turn to Anne Lamott to say things I know but can't explain, 'Forgiveness means it finally becomes unimportant that you hit back.' Then again, being chronically human and all that jazz, by the time I forgive something I'll probably have some new grudges to work on.

Sometimes blame can be incredibly satisfying. Like blaming former lovers or the right wing or the fact that your mother or father or third grade teacher didn't love you enough. You can blame all of your dysfunctions on someone else or you can just get over it and learn to move the fuck on.

Learn to walk away, this is one of the roughest lessons I've had to learn so far. Sometimes even though it hurts you just have to know when to say enough is enough with people. Just walk away, even though it might feel good to tell them in great detail what a ratty person they are or to teach them a lesson. Delete their number from your phone. Don't answer their calls or emails. Don't meet them anywhere 'just one last time'. As the Beetles say, let it be. Then again, a little anonymous revenge can also be very therapeutic to the soul.

Mon coeur est brise mais il bat encore.
My heart is broken but it still beats.
So it goes.

Kaitlyn Jane Mauro

Hatchling.

'Hope is the thing with feathers
That perches in the soul,
And sings the tune - without the words,
And never stops at all'
(Emily Dickinson)

I bought a book of Emily Dickinson's poetry and I fell instantly in love with these lines. Page twenty-two, a lovely number. Tonight I found a baby blue jay while I was at work. A crow snatched him out of his nest in the trees and left him on the pavement. I felt heartsick for him - so young his feathers hadn't even grown in yet. He would breath so rapidly, then so slowly it was barely detectable at all. I didn't know what to do with him while I waited for my shift at the cafe to end so I put him in one of our to-go boxes with a napkin nest and left him next to the employee exit. Every fifteen minutes or so I would slip away and run back to check if he was still alive. I'd be relieved to see his little birdie chest rising and falling, then worry for the next fifteen minutes until I could go check on him again. I don't know why I decided he was a him, he just seemed like a little him I suppose. I probably mixed up quite a few orders that night while my mind was on other things.

Four hours later I was finally done working and he was still alive so I took him home with me in his little Via Panera catering box. I kept him warm and fed him moistened kitten food like the animal rehabilitation center told me to. He didn't look too good.

Don't worry, it will happen differently anyway.

Maybe in heaven I'll sing with a little more soul.

There is something mesmerizing about people who can play the piano beautifully. I have several friends who have been playing for most of their lives. When I watch them I always feel like their fingers are some kind of magical, dancing out notes and melodies. It's just more proof to me that God exists, how we can tell the difference between a bunch of notes and music. Where do these instincts come from? It's all too sincere. I love to lean back and close my eyes, humming gently along. I like the delicate, haunting pieces best. I hate bagpipes and organs, they sound so tactless and invasive. Like an extra loud relative obliviously embarrassing himself in public. I try to see, smell, and taste the sounds I hear. Never stop searching for new angles.

And I'm not going back
Into rags or in the hole
And our bruises are coming
But we will never fold

Sometimes my friends teach me how to play little melodies when we're sitting by the piano together. For some reason I am too shy to sing in front of most people, even my friends. Last night I was at my old church sitting in the sanctuary alone at the piano. The big room with it's cathedral ceilings and aisles of stone columns was in perfect darkness except for the small light next to me. I was just playing around, amusing myself by singing along with my fingers as they danced clumsily over the ivory keys. Sometimes being alone is lovely.

Then, from the back of the sanctuary my friend says, 'You have a beautiful voice, you know.' I nearly jumped out of my skin. I had known there were other people in the church but

I couldn't see him at all. He had tiptoed through the back doors while I hadn't been paying attention and had just been sitting there listening to me. I felt a little embarrassed to be caught with my guard completely down like that. His words made me blush.

And I was your silver lining
High up on my toes
I was your silver lining
But now - I'm gold.

There is something intimate about being seen when you think you are alone. Even when you aren't exactly in private, maybe you just think nobody has noticed you then you realize you have an audience. It's like they are seeing your most authentic self, without any make up or emotional barriers.

The lyrics are from Silver Lining by Rilo Kiley. Someday I will fall in love to this song.

Hurray Hurray
I'm your silver lining
Hurray Hurray
But now – I'm gold

Kaitlyn Jane Mauro

My darling baby blue jay died during the night. My eyes played tricks on me when I went to check on him this morning. At first I thought he was breathing and my heart fluttered. Then I looked more closely and realized he was perfectly still. What a sad start to the day.

Rubber tramps and that wanderlust feeling.

Well, I've just gotten back from my long awaited (read: obsessively anticipated) road trip with my sister. It was amazing. We spent two weeks on the road, watching the scenery change as we drove all the way from Austin, Texas to the coast of California. I've always had a chronic case of wanderlust. I have a terrible time answering when people ask me 'If you could live anywhere in the world where would you choose?' because I wouldn't pick anywhere. I would live like a nomad and wake up in a different place each week. It was a special trip too because my sister is getting married and graduating from college next summer - this may have been one of the last chances for us to bond like this. I wasn't used to the southwestern sun and got a pretty impressive sunburn on day one.

-

(From the travel notebooks:)

I have so much to write about, even though we've barely even begun our trip. Jump skip hop - my mind is all over the place, there is too much to be inspired by. We left on our adventure yesterday at 5:45am, getting vanilla iced coffee (my new addiction) then spending the rest of the day driving through Western Texas. I knew Texas was big but this was just ridiculous. So much empty space. We started in Austin, near the middle of the state, and it *still* took us hours and hours and hours to get to the New Mexico border - even with the 85mph speed limit most of the way. I took about a million pictures of the mountains and the scenery, it's so different from my Pennsylvania. I love that there is so much variety.

We didn't stop again until we got to El Paso. El Paso was scary, to say things simply. I think we would have felt fine about it except before we left everyone tried to warn Kim and me with cautionary tales about things that happen down by the border. Either way, it worked out. We found a little vegetarian café in one of my travel books and had a very late lunch. We parked the car where we could see it.

Some jazzy things that have happened today - I saw Mexico while we were driving by. Then we got stopped by border patrol. 'You ladies citizens?' they asked with heavy Spanish accents. We said we were and they let us drive away. A while later we drove through a 'time zone barrier'. Doesn't that sound incredibly geeky and science fiction-like? We had the sunroof down and were singing along to the radio, classic road trip moments.

That evening we reached our first destination: White Sands, New Mexico. It was the perfect way to end our first day of traveling. We thought we'd missed it or taken the wrong road because to get there you drive for miles and miles and miles through red-brown dessert, past little towns and superstores and nothing space. Then, out of the blue, there are giant sand dunes on either side of you that stretch as far as you can see. It looks a little like the beach, except you are in the middle of the desert and everything is dry as a bone. It's not like ocean sand, all tanned and gritty and speckled. These dunes are pure white, they look snow but are hot as pavement. In the pictures we took it looks like we're standing in the middle of winter but there are desert plants in the corners that give us away. They're massive too, towering stories above the ground. They are called 'Gypsum' sand dunes because of the minerals that form them. I think 'gypsum' is a really beautiful word, it fit the place perfectly. Like gypsies - spinning and foreign and colorful. The dunes are over 7,000 years old and are constantly changing and moving as the wind blows the sand from place to place.

As the sun set we sat on the dunes with scattered groups of our fellow travelers. Travelers really are my favorite kind of people, they are so full of stories and interested in life (which, in turn, makes them interesting). They aren't afraid of new things, they stop to smell the flowers. We all waited and watched the sky turn lavenders and pale pearl pinks, like the pearly tones on the inside of a sea shell, as the sun disappeared behind the distant line of the mountains. After a while it was nearly dark and people wandered back to their cars, talking quietly. The desert felt sacred in the dark, like a church or a library, and everyone felt it. My sister and I were the last people there because she was trying to capture every last image and angle with her camera before the light was entirely gone.

'I travel not to go anywhere but to go. I travel for travel's sake. The great affair is to move.'
(Robert Louis Stevenson)

'The great affair is to move', que bonita. As we were shaking the sand out of our shoes and clothes, preparing for our drive to Albuquerque where we would stay for the night, the sky abruptly changed again. We were taken aback because the 'sunset' had already occurred, we'd all sat there and watched it. Now the sky and the ridges of the mountains were on fire, violets, pinks, yellows, reds, and gold. It changed from minute to minute, like watercolors seeping into fabric - mixing together and forming new hues. Set against the blank canvas of the white sand it was one of the most magnificent sights I had ever seen. Nobody has prepared us for this, I feel so sorry for the people who had already left and unknowingly missed the real thing.

-

Today while driving we passed a big, wooden sign that proclaimed 'Welcome to Colorful Colorado!' I looked over at my sister and she looked at me. 'Colorado? Why the hell would we be in Colorado?' Silence. I reach for the maps.

-

We have seen so many things in the past five days! It's amazing when you think about how much there really is to see, even just in this one country. We are 2,500 miles into our trip and have just reached California! I have always wanted to be here. It's just as beautiful as I'd imagined. I love how they have flowers growing on the highway dividers.

-

(Some things we've done so far...)

Seen Natural Bridges Park. Watched the sun rise and set over the Grand Canyon. Mastered the puzzle that is putting up our tent. Spent two nights camping on the edge of the Grand Canyon. Seen more stars than I ever have in my life. Almost gotten sprayed by a skunk. Stood ten feet away from a huge wild Elk. Met tons of other road trippers. Seen Monument Valley. Attempted to cook with a propane stove. Bought turquoise jewelry on the streets of Santa Fe. Gone to Zion National Park. Met a lot of hippies. Accidentally hiked the 'advanced' trail to the Emerald Pool. Stood at the top of the waterfall and looked over. Stayed in some very shady motels. Lived off of iced coffee and granola bars. Dipped my toes in the Pacific Ocean for the first time. Driven a hundred miles without seeing another soul. Stood ten feet away from a rattle snake! Been soaked by rain in Santa Monica. Seen the wind blow 'waves of amber grain' across the great plains. Driven on crazy cliff roads two feet from a clear drop off of several thousand feet - no guard rails. Saved a baby rabbit. Spontaneously went to Las Vegas. Ate at the biggest P.F. Chang's ever. Went to the M&M and Coca-Cola factories. Filled my camera's memory card. Stayed at a giant hotel made entirely of glass.

-

It's strange to travel to a place you have seen a hundred times but only in photographs. I always find myself, in some silly way, feeling surprised that it really exists. It seems miraculous that it is here, taking up space and existing in hours the same way I am. Kind of like meeting someone famous and feeling silly for somehow almost feeling surprised they really exist. I had seen so many pictures of the Grand Canyon but pictures really can't do something that enormous and beautiful justice. If you've been there you understand.

My other favorite destination came near the end of our trip, before we reached the coast of California - the Giant Sequoia Forests. The trees are so massive that when one fell down they carved a tunnel and people drive their RV's through. It's amazing. I felt a little like Alice when she drinks the shrinking potion and finds herself so tiny in Wonderland. My favorite was a tree that was over two thousand years old. I stood there and thought of all the things that have happened and changed in the past two thousand years. All the people that have lived and died, all the things that have gone on in other parts of the world. I thought of Jesus' birth and Marie Antoinette, the Boston Tea Party and Kennedy's Assassination. The tree was there, rooted in the soil for it all. It made history feel nearer, more tangible.

*'I travel a lot; I hate having my life
disrupted by routine.'*
(Caskie Stinnett)

I love traveling by air, even if the news lately is nearly enough to scare me out of it. The flight attendant on the way home was really sweet, she had a bit of an accent and kept calling me 'bella'. I wonder where she was from. Back to the daily grind.

Kaitlyn Jane Mauro

Eating grapes off the wallpaper:

'I am aiming to be somebody that somebody trusts - oh but sensible sounds would you kindly shut up? … With a delicate soul I don't claim to know much.'
(Bottle It Up, Sara Barellies)

Some man shot his wife in a McDonald's in Bedford yesterday. People are so messed up sometimes. I wonder what they were even fighting about. Probably love - or maybe money. I could be perfectly happy in life creating and seeking out the loveliness in unexpected places. I do I do I do.

Sometimes when life becomes boring I make myself imagine everything as more significant than it really is. Sometimes I get too intense and I ask too many questions. Sometimes I'm too shy to apologize even when the sentence is on the tip of my tongue. I'll forget to filter my words, I say things too bluntly. Touch my hand and I'll believe you are listening. Remember when we held hands the whole way home and didn't need to speak a word, it was just enough? Some people claim they have no regrets in life. I am definitely not one of these people.

I heard if you can resist the urge to breath drowning is one of the least painful ways to go and I heard when you starve the hunger fades after the first couple of days. I wonder if it's true.

I scared myself today while I was driving home from rehearsal. I kept thinking about what would happen if I just turned the steering wheel and let my car spin off the road. I couldn't ever do this - my mom needs this car. But the thought kept creeping in, tempting me. I played out a million little scenarios in my mind. When I got home I called a friend I have known since kindergarten and he cheered me up and even made me laugh. Laughter makes everything feel less terminal.

A couple months ago I painted the words *'ne jamais prendre la vie trop au serioux'* on my wall. It means something along the lines of 'never take life too seriously' in French. I don't take French (yet) so I'm sure this is a grammatical train wreck, but in the end it really couldn't matter less. Cory tells me the 'au' isn't necessary but it just looks so *French...* I left it anyway. I still can't seem to remember this line when I really need it.

'My baby wants bad things
She's stuck in the middle of her labyrinth.
Small hope for the quick unwind
But now I've come to find:
That she's a lion in disguise.'
(Yucatan Gold, Throw Me The Statue)

I never write on the first page of a new notebook, it's too much pressure. Like whatever you put there sets the tone for all the other pages. I like to keep my options open.

I heard an interesting concept the other day, something I want to remember. It was something along the lines of emotions are only feelings and neither the good ones or the bad ones can be counted on to last. The bottom-line is we can't control how we feel, we can only control our actions. I feel like people with eating disorders understand this better than the rest of us, they just take it way too far. If we want to be *something* then we have to start acting like whatever it is. For example, if you want to be a great student, then start acting like a great student. If you want to be thin, then start behaving as thin person would. If you want to be a writer then start acting like a writer. It makes total sense but I had never thought about it so simply before. Cause and effect, the simplest answer is usually the right one.

I feel I feel I feel. It's so repetitive.

New goal for myself: random acts of kindness everyday. I don't understand what any of us is living for. My past is a graveyard of plans, mistakes, and goals that have come and gone like the weather. New dreams replace the old.

I am teaching myself a second language trying not to let him into my thoughts. There's no sound for him in these new words, no sentences that once belonged to us.

Untitled.

God I hate this room. The muted colors and the smell, like fresh paint and sanitizing spray and office. I try to make a list in my head of places I would like to be even less than here. Nothing comes to mind. Stomach twisting. I feel light, like my bones have become as hollow as a bird's. I could almost fly away. I feel my heart beating beneath my ribs. The rhythm feels more pronounced than usual. I'm at the hospital, sitting and waiting like they always have you do before doctor's appointments - even when you show up on time.

Louis Louis
Please come back to the quiet generation
We don't have any representation
Louis Louis

It's not like anything legitimately bad ever happens to me here. The anxiety this place stirs is completely unreasonable - but knowing and recognizing that fact doesn't make it any less real. That's the nature of irrational fears. I actually like my doctor a lot. She's smart and down to earth and has a little tattoo on the inside of her left wrist. A Chinese symbol, I ask her the meaning. The thing is, these appointments never turn out well. The numbers are always too high and there is always the same, miserable conversation on the way home. We've been following this script for years.

Louis Louis
Our stars no longer shine
Louis Louis
Come down through the heavens

The earliest memory I can recall is getting having the flu when I was quite young, maybe four years old. I had already been diagnosed with diabetes several years before which is where the phobia of all things medical began. In this memory my mother is carrying me in and out of the kitchen in the house on Windsor Ave where I grew up. It was just starting to get dark outside. She's trying to convince me to eat. Something, anything - I remember her offering applesauce and I said I would have some but the weight of it in my mouth made me nauseous. There was a pleading tone to her voice. She said if I didn't eat something we would have to go back to the hospital. Nobody wanted that, not them and definitely not me but eating just wasn't an option. Back to the hospital we went.

The sky is full of innuendos
We don't want any heroes
Louis Louis

I remember a room with circus scene wallpaper and being strapped to a table. They couldn't get an IV line going because the veins in my arm were too small. The memories come in little snippets and snapshots - the smell of the room and the alcohol sanitizing wipes, the colorful, childish patterns of the nurse's scrubs and the wallpaper. It's funny how the wallpaper is what I remember most clearly. Elephants and circus tents and a tiger.

Louis Louis
They shot all the poets
Louis Louis
The world is not like you know it

I love that verse.
The song is Louis Louis by Teitur.

Flash forward to third grade. I slide a kitchen chair over to the wall where our family calendar hangs and run my finger along the little boxes, trying to decipher my mother's messy, adult handwriting. I do this every so often, scanning for appointments. Usually they are marked with my name and a time or the word 'children's'. When my mother started catching onto my antics she would mark them with only a letter 'C'. Once I found one written in pencil and erased it while my mother was on the phone, distracted. I thought if it wasn't on the calendar she would most likely forget about it and we wouldn't have to go. It almost worked until I learned they call a few days before your appointment to confirm.

There's no one with the right agenda
That's why we stay down here
And want to surrender
Louis Louis

Sometimes it's like that feeling of panic never left, something will trigger the memories and it will come right back up like it has only been hibernating. Even when I'm only visiting someone else in a hospital I feel flighty and anxious. One time I had to go to the hospital with a friend because he needed stitches and I thought I was going to pass out just from the colors and the smells. My pulse drums and my stomach curls. Mind over matter - I am finally starting to get the hang of this. Cold blood will stop you dead in your tracks.

Kaitlyn Jane Mauro

Love is a dangerous past time.

It's nearly six in the morning and I don't know why I'm still awake. At this point I almost want to just stay up and wait for the sun to rise, then I will sleep for a few hours before my lunch date with this boy. It's all still so strange, after two years of exchanging sweet words with the same person, to be making dates with new people and starting over with the awkward moments and the same get-to-know-you questions - with the excitement of the new. It's all so innocent again, we play the part with good intentions but bad romances leave you with scraped palms and bruised knees.

I like tall boys with accents or men with cynical senses of humor who know about politics and the world. It's funny how my tastes have shifted recently.

One thing that's strange to look back on is how the groups of people who make up your days change over time. People who mean the world to you one summer are like strangers the next. Sometimes quieting slipping out, other times leaving painful empty spaces or wreckage in their wake. Half the kids I know have divorced parents. I think this happens because everyone is always changing. We feel hurt when someone we love evolves into a different person over the years but we are all constantly doing it too. Nobody means their wedding vows. Nobody makes the effort to stay in love. I heard that marriage is falling in love over and over again, just with the same person.

-

I woke up at four o'clock this morning for no particular reason. It was dark when I started writing but the sky is a beautiful shade of lilac blue now, the exact color of hydrangeas. It's been snowing all week. Yesterday I looked out the window and saw my sister's pony in the field behind our house - the snow was so high you couldn't see his legs at all. He was just glossy black wading through the white. It was a pretty funny sight. Noelle is laying with her head on my lap, I love watching her sides rise and fall as she breathes. A hot mug of tea sounds just right at the moment.

Listen to 'Heart It Races' by Dr. Dog and 'Strange Bird' by Kelsey Wild. A friend burned these onto a mix cd she made me; absolutely lovely.

'Sometimes I wish I could just hum along to piano music and never have to search for the right words ever again.' I can't remember when but my friend Brittney said this once. It has really stuck with me for some reason. She says things so beautifully sometimes. I don't understand how anyone could read her writing and not fall instantly in love with such a person.

Kaitlyn Jane Mauro

You taste like glitter mixed with rock n roll.

Ten O'clock. I started anew.

Today has been so average. How sad, such a waste. 'Make every day extraordinary'. God, I need to try harder. I spent a bit of today studying but most of it reading. Nothing substantial, but it left me hungry for life. I had forgotten how lovely it is to write with a real pen and paper, to not worry about grammar or sounding lyrical, only about saying what you need to say. My handwriting looks unfamiliar, like it belongs to someone else - maybe someone I used to know. There are so many things in life I want to do but for some reason I feel paralyzed by fear - what are we all so afraid of? I want to run away to the west coast and live near the sea. I want to get another tattoo but I have no idea what to get. Maybe something about love or God. I don't even feel God anymore. I can barely remember what it was like to have faith like a child, to not care if any of it made logical sense. Nothing makes sense this year anyway.

-

I dated a boy named Tyler back when I was just a freshman in high school. There were actually two Tylers that year, right in a row. This is the second. We met in the theater and he was a total womanizer. I was bright eyed and naïve, slipping easily under his spells. I fall fast, it's just a fact. It's not love, I just love the concept of being in love. It's the curse of the romantics. People like Tyler don't suffer from these heart related problems. I think the fact I recognize it isn't the real thing is what saves me most of the time. The funny part is that I think the only boy I ever really loved was the one I never dated. We could have broken all the rules.

I digress, back to Tyler. He wasn't even exceptionally tall or interesting. Looking back I can't understand why all of the girls fell for him.

It must have been his slippery charm. All of the freshman girls liked him at least, the older girls saw right through him. I am one of those older girls now, no longer so optimistic and innocent. Hindsight's 20/20 they say. A boy I've known my whole life says this is because I've become a bitch. The naïve, insecure freshman he dates are not bitches, 'they're sweet'. I've noticed men like to label a woman who disagrees with them or look out for herself a 'bitch'. Maybe I should take this as a compliment. I am only thinking about Tyler now because I saw his picture on someone's facebook page yesterday. He's gained a lot of weight and had a big, furry cat sitting on his shoulder... It made me smile. Try to stay wide-eyed.

-

My self esteem is suffering a little this week because I decided to drop one of my classes. It wasn't important or required, oh well. This semester was supposed to be more relaxed, my last one at home. I am both scared and excited at the thought of moving away and living on my own. I have mixed feelings about staying in this city. Long term I know I won't. Someday I'll runaway, leaving only a note on the kitchen table. I hate goodbyes anyway. I'll adopt a new name and start fresh, born hungry. I want to live in so many different places. That sentence could almost be 'I want to live so many different lives.'

-

'Art is the only way to runaway
without leaving home.'
(Twyla Tharp)

Je Suis En Forme.

I have just begun studying French and this is my favorite sentence, so far at least. It's a response to 'ca va?' (how are you?) that translates something like 'I am in form.' It reminds me of ballet and feels beautiful and airy on my lips. Kind of like 'I'm still breathing'. My heart is still beating. I can still get out of bed in the morning and pretend to function like a normal human being. I can still accomplish. We're all alright, as they sing on That 70's Show. What a gift to have our heartbeats to constantly remind us that we are alive. Tick tock tick tock. Time is slipping through my fingers. I waste days and accomplish nothing. I am not even out of high school yet and I feel old, like I've missed too many opportunities and my body can't dance like it used to. Life is so short. Just breath, we are all still so young. I wish I could turn up the volume on my heartbeat so I would always hear it in the back of my mind. I would never forget that each day is numbered. I spend embarrassing amounts of time wondering what people would say about me if I died in some tragic manner. I think we all secretly do it.

Writing my letters puts me in a strange mood. Like there is so much to say and no words, no way to express it. I don't really understand why it happens. I don't know how to describe it. I've found several new pen pals lately so I've been doing a lot of listening and a lot of telling. I love decorating the envelopes with images cut out from fashion magazines or quotes I've gathered. I collect quotes everywhere I go and scribble them on yellow post it notes, the wall by my desk is covered.

I want to become such a great listener. Listeners are such a rare find. I hate how in our conversations we are only pretending to care while we wait for our turn to speak. I hate how we only ask a question so we can tell our own answer. I want to look into your eyes and soak in every word and inflection.

Something about today is just so beautiful it's breaking my heart. I can't quite put my finger on it. When I woke up this morning I felt like I could fall in love with absolutely everything. It's the craziest feeling. Maybe it's because I am running scared. Nothing feels real to me, there are too many choices to be made. God, all I want is to travel. We build our own cages and then sing about the freedom we've been denied.

I don't want romantic sweet nothings or sugary valentines day cards or heartfelt poetry. I don't want fancy dates or big ceremonies or cliché promises. Tell me something so genuine and wrought with truth that it brings me to my knees and I'm yours. Let's not try to solve everything in one night.

I can't watch the news today.

Kaitlyn Jane Mauro

As we're escaping, ghosts of the past sleep lightly, so mind the floorboards.

I adore something about that quote. I love when people wear peach and gold together, or black nylons with brightly colored lipstick. Chipped nail polish is so charming. It says, 'I care about beauty and the little things but I'm too busy living life to be a perfectionist. I don't take myself too seriously.' I could fall in love with your every word.

There is a box in the basement I'm afraid to open. When I finally grew sober of him I put all the love letters, pictures, and memories in a box and put them out of my room, into the basement. It made the air easier to breath; these things will haunt you if you keep them in your drawers. I needed space to rid him from my bones.

There are a lot of emotions in that box - a lot of beautiful firsts and a lot of lies. Writing brings these things up. I've noticed something that worries me - my creativity is much stronger when my heart is broken. I think I understand why Sylvia Plath stuck her head in the oven. I think I understand what my friend meant when I asked her why she did it and she said 'to feel'. I have been feeling uninspired lately and part of me is tempted to open that box and to let the pain come back so I can find a reason to create. But I won't, not this week - because I'm afraid one of these times when I'm pulled under I won't be able to pull myself back out. Let sleeping dogs lie.

"For the poet is an airy thing, a winged and a holy thing; she cannot make poetry until she becomes inspired and goes out of her senses and no mind is left in her."
(Plato)

Sometimes I'll have a moment when I'll realize how incredibly alone we all really are. It brings me to my knees. These are the moments when I pray. Not when things are going well but when I've run out of things to try. 'Help help help help help' - Anne Lamott says it is the great helping prayer. I find it's the one I use most frequently. The other one is probably 'why why why why why'.

Total Silence, No answer
But the best thing God has created
Is a new day
(Sigur Ros)

Brittney wrote these lyrics on the envelope of the first letter she wrote me. Sigur Ros makes some of the most beautiful music I've ever heard.

Soon I will remember how to breathe and if I'm lucky the sun will come up soon or the stars will be out. Change your clothes and make some tea, put on some mascara. We can survive anything. I'm waiting for the worst one yet.

What if I never ever met you?
What if we never fell in love?
What if we kept on singing love songs?
Just to break our own hearts?
(Regina Spektor)

Kaitlyn Jane Mauro

Sensory Overload, Question Everything

My perspective is never right. It swings between the extremes. Either so big nothing matters and I'm completely apathetic or too small and I'm overwhelmed by every little detail. Everything becomes a blur. Shrinking and expanding, like the baby blue veins under our skin. I'm in a weird mood tonight. Sometimes thinking about things too much does that to you. I'll tuck myself into bed soon. We're working towards balance. Six pills tonight, I don't feel a thing.

I wish I could pick a new name, something eccentric and memorable that flows like champagne. Celebrities do it all the time, change their names to match their personas. It's all marketing. I'm named for my grandmother. Tonight my mind is skipping beats all over the place. I can't follow a train of thought but I can't sleep either. Excellent.

When I read I write all over the pages. I crack the spine and bend back the corners. I hope you read this book like that. I bought a book called Wreck This Journal when the leaves were changing color. It's all about freeing your inner creativity by getting past the big sense of guilty perfectionism we all inadvertently hold onto. Each page has a different set of instructions for something you are supposed to do to the book. One page asked me to poke holes all through it with a sharpened pencil. Another told me to rip the page right out, to crinkle it up and send it through the washing machine with my favorite pair of jeans.

It sounds crazy but it's liberating. Like that scene in Dead Poet's Society when the Mr. Keating has them rip the introduction out of their textbooks in protest. You can't judge poetry with a passionless grading scale. It's something you have to feel. The struggle between the realists and the romantics will probably never end. 'That the powerful play goes on and you may contribute a verse,' one of my favorite lines from that film. Such brilliance.

I love people watching and I'm infatuated with birds. It was all true at one moment or another.

-

I've just gotten a second tattoo - a little bird on my left shoulder blade. It was a spontaneous decision. She's black with a touch of blue highlighting her wings. The sparrow is the sailor's symbol, the sign of the traveler. She represents the ability to adapt and a higher spirituality. She represents constant change and buoyancy. The world is my home, not one address or city or even country. I never regret my tattoos because they become a part of me. Besides, when you think about it, life really isn't that long anyway - the commitment is marginal.

-

'Out of the ash
I rise with my red hair
And I eat men like air'
(Sylvia Plath)

Sylvia Plath's son killed himself today. I can't pull myself out of the water this week. Things between Christopher and I are weird. Our words are empty and passionless, it's almost over. I hate when things become boring but it's the natural close to this mess. I'm doing everything wrong lately. The news is scary and I feel panicky. Fuck it, I don't have the energy to care.

While I was on break at work I heard a lady in the booth next to mine say, 'my heart is completely shut down.' What a tragedy. My heart is set on nowhere. I am committing my life to wandering and experiencing as much as I can.

-

I have a hard choice to make right now: stay where I am comfortable or move someplace new, risking the unknown. I already know what I will choose. I'll go, because it's who I am. It's okay because I don't truly think we are soul mates, even though you told me we were. If you mean it at the time, is it still a lie? I meant it all when the words left my lips - but things change and it hurts but it's the only way life could be. I couldn't survive stagnancy. We'll both fall again.

I'm starving for some adventure and human contact.

'Whatever is true, whatever is noble, whatever is right, whatever is pure, whatever is lovely, whatever is admirable - if anything is excellent or praiseworthy - think about such things.' A verse from the bible I really like, even though I am generally not a huge fan of the bible. It's Philippians 4:8.

I want to expand my vocabulary and learn to skip meals. I will occupy myself with beautiful things. We are all constant works in progress, as long as you keep trying your head stays above the water.

-

Whoever comes are the right people and whatever happens is the only thing that could have. Words to live by.

'I never think of the future,
it comes soon enough.'
- Albert Einstein

One could drown in irrelevance.

'The best thing about the future is that it only comes one day at a time.'
(Abraham Lincoln)

'Any idiot can face a crisis, it's the day to day living that wears you out.'
(Anton Chekhov)

Such conflicting messages. They're both true. It matters but at the same time it's all completely irrelevant. We constantly contradict ourselves. Tonight my family (or what's left of it) was sitting down to do the one thing we all do together these days - watch American Idol. My mother was eating some fudge twirl ice cream right out of the carton. We are big fans of doing that in my house. Casey, the youngest of my sisters, who looks just like me and is rather precocious, looked at my mother and said 'Mom, you are going to get fat'. 'But what a way to go,' my mother responded. I could love her just for saying this.

Unfinished thoughts. Unfinished thoughts.

> 'To live a creative life,
> we must lose our fear of being wrong.'
> (Joseph Chilton Pearce)

So much of my writing begins or ends with 'I feel', but feelings will only get you so far and, in the end, they are only worth so much consideration. The truth is very few people will care anyway.

On the bright side, I am done painting my bathroom. There are splotches of lavender paint on my thighs and my face. I need to get back into the habit of writing my letters.

-

Five cops were shot in my city yesterday. Three of them died on the scene. They were just doing some routine visit, going to a domestic argument to tell them to hush down. The crazy had a military rifle and decided he had the right to end their lives. I feel terrible for their families. Hearing these things in the morning always throws my day into grey. People are so fragile.

Some days it feels like such a fine line - it's more 'functional' or 'dysfunctional' than 'crazy' or 'sane'. I could start screaming and not even recognize the sound as my own. I could possibly never stop. I am so tired of trying to explain myself. There are so many ways to look at everything. Everything is true and everything is a lie.

Kaitlyn Jane Mauro

Tea with honey, por favor.

*"What we have here folks is a dreamer, someone
completely out of touch with reality. When she
jumped she probably thought she could fly."*
(The Virgin Suicides)

I notice my writing changing from chapter
to chapter. I think It's tragic how we are always
going back to re-question people's motives. We
tell each other who we are in all sorts of quiet
ways. People are so beautiful sometimes, I love
seeing them in their most human moments, it's
incredibly likable. I want to take apart each little

characteristic, I'm trying to understand what we are made of. Fate is such a sticky concept.

Driving to my art class today I randomly felt more alive and free than I have in days. I love when these moods of inspiration come, reminding me what I am living for. I turned up the classical station and let the music surround me. I tried to absorb it right into my core, to use all of my senses. Warm air blew on my face and fingers from the vents. In art class we learned how to use the old fashioned giant of a printing press, turning the wheel like we're steering a ship. I love the systematic mess of the studio. People hang their prints all over the walls and lay them on every flat surface to dry. Everything is colorful, our hands are splattered with paint. I love to make art just for the sake of creating.

'I love strange choices. I'm always interested in people who depart from what is expected of them and go into new territory.'
(Cate Blanchett)

The postal guy came this morning, his arms stacked high with square white boxes - my textbooks for this new semester. I'm feeling mildly overwhelmed by it all, sometimes this almost seems like a state of being. My room desperately needs to be cleaned, I want to buy fresh flowers for my desk. Winter can be so tedious. I need to mark dates on the calendar and organize myself. I'll feel better once I get a start on it. Tomorrow I become an early bird - up at six o'clock.

We are constantly putting things off, saying 'someday I will try this, someday I will accomplish that, eventually I will become A or develop the habit of B'? I have no more patience for wasted days, I am done waiting.

Kaitlyn Jane Mauro

I fall a little bit in love with every person I meet.

One Six Billionth

Kaitlyn Jane Mauro

One Six Billionth

Kaitlyn Jane Mauro

Much deserved gratitude and hugs to the following people...

Mom and Dad: for everything. What haven't you done?

Nana and Poppy: for all the lunch dates, listening, letting me take over the guest room, and basically being a second set of parents.

Kim, Kevin, Colleen, and Casey: because we survived this growing up thing together. I love you all, no matter where we all end up.

Brittney Lewis: for letting me borrow her lovely photography talents for the cover, being a wonderful friend, and all the letters and constant inspiration.

Kaitlyn Jane Mauro

The Author

This is Kaitlyn Jane's first published work. She is currently jumping through hoops to finish her last semester of high school and resides with her family in Western Pennsylvania - but not for long. She adores spontaneity, iced coffee, books, traveling, foreign languages, and interesting people. Bonsoir!

Kaitlyn Jane Mauro

One Six Billionth

Kaitlyn Jane Mauro

One Six Billionth

This is not the end…

Kaitlyn Jane Mauro

...It is not even the beginning of the end...

Kaitlyn Jane Mauro

One Six Billionth

...But it is, perhaps,
the end of the beginning.
(Winston Churchill)

Kaitlyn Jane Mauro

Made in the USA
Charleston, SC
07 February 2010